23 summers of sarra

Jenna Youse Ragsdale

BookLeaf
Publishing

Presentation by *BookLeaf Publishing*

Web: www.bookleafpub.com

E-mail: info@bookleafpub.com

ISBN: 9789395621076

First edition 2022

DEDICATION

23 Summers of Sarra is dedicated to my fallen forever friend, Sarra Josephine. In her 23 years of life, she taught me what it means to be a woman, a friend, and always reminded me and those around her to enjoy every second of life to the fullest.

ACKNOWLEDGEMENT

Thank you to my Mom, Dad, my sister, Amy, and my Aunt Tina for supporting me in every way—especially my poetry.

Thank you to my loving supportive husband, Vaughn, for being my partner in life, and constantly showing enthusiasm for all my endeavors.

A special thank you to my longest friend, Dayna Smedley, for re-reading, editing my poetry, and pushing me to follow my dreams.

Finally, I thank my dear friends Nikki Russo, Morgan Mountz, and Kelsey Hartell for their continued support, and endless belly-laughs!

PREFACE

Life is hard and it will take our entire lives to even get an inkling of figuring it out. Over the years I have learned there is healing in knowing that showing your emotions and sharing your own stories makes you a more relatable person and let's face it: no one wants to feel alone.

In my 23 Summers of Sarra, I magnify moments in our lives that make us all part of the human race. Whether it's taking time to appreciate the minute lessons along the way, falling in love, or sharing the many instances when it's hard to be a woman, I want to connect with the reader in every way possible. I want the reader to reflect on their own lives and relate to my poems so that they can reevaluate or commend themselves on all they have accomplished in life until this point.

I aim to prove to the reader how valid and important their feelings, viewpoints, and thoughts are and ask them to appreciate and honor themselves in a world that's constantly asking them to compare themselves to everyone else. We are all important and worthy of love, friendship, and healing, and it is time we all start to realize that!

golden

don't waste your golden years
wondering if they're golden or not.
don't forget who you are—
for you've been golden all along.

aye yi yi

you have to laugh
at the irony of men
telling us to smile
when they're the ones
causing all the disappointments

indescribable but still, i try

like 5 PM on a Friday night
sprinting out of work
fresh air slaps my face,
making my hair dance
as fireworks unexpectedly
explode at your family's
frequented beach,
awakening all your senses
beaming warm sun-rays
blanketing my entirety.
i get chills day-dreaming
of sweet salty summer,
the first bite of pizza,
stars strung on strings
strategically set up in the sky
just for us. sing-a-long
road-trips flying by,
sunday dinners & everyone
could make it this week
like your favorite ride having
no line & all the christmas lights
lighting up in unison on the tree
without checking beforehand.
i smell chocolate-chip cookies
coming out of the oven &
jack frost claymation starts to play—
yeah, that is how you make me feel.

my backyard

i remember when i was young
thinking my backyard
was the entire world.
i also remember
feeling my heart
sink
the shattering second
i realized it was not.

grandmother/mother/aunt/dau ghter

my body carries suspended bricks
of inherited insecurities
my bones ache from the world's weight
stacking up against us
my fingertips encase red threads
used to stitch our aunt's lips,
in spite of their innocence—
my legs, tree-stumps, planting in
places i never planned on journeying
my heart, encapsulated in stony gravel,
in hopes to protect what's left
for our future daughters
my hips hold the history of our heritage,
broad, strong & built to last
my voice, raspy & raw—echoing whispers
of wisdom from our mothers,
she has laid our foundations
she has told us to keep both
sets of our lips clenched, & that
we must love one another
we must help one another
we must scream for one another—
for there is no silencing of mother nature's
wishes

intimacy

in the end
we all want it
we're born longing for it—
someone to listen
someone to leave the light on
someone to surprise us with forehead kisses
someone who studies our eyes like lighthouses
swept up in smog—
to make sure our compass is on course—
the truest form of intimacy

untied

i untied the angry weights
that pinned me down,
no wonder i felt so stuck.
i popped the hate balloons,
burst into ugly cries—
a loud blubbery mess.
floating in a forgiving feeling,
i inhale/exhale—i've never
breathed this deep before

ruby bushes

the warm wet rose
blooming without notice
the red gushing geyser
flowing freely between our legs
the fountain of foundation
enduring painful intrusions,
interruptions & invasions
& ridiculed no matter the landscape
& treatments of our bloody
thorny protections by our
garden bushes, & still—
they pierce us
they cut us
they prune us
having no idea
their rust cannot excavate
our rubies, for they are not
up for the taking &
they never will be

intentional

everyone's had
their heart-punched
& their soul-sink-holed.
release your past & celebrate the future;
for you are not here by accident.
you deserve the stars, the sun &
you need to believe it—for they dance
for those unafraid to see.

the woman

i admit
i was lost
floated away
took foolish chances
wasted years that i took for
granted; sadness swallowed me whole
every weekend i had to go on apology tours
but then came my 30s & the fog started
fading—how lucky am i to get an act II? i'm
finally finding the woman my mom raised me to
be

takers

silly me
to think giving you
parts of me
would make you feel whole
now i'm left limbless
while you bloom
under someone else's sun

home plate

nothing compares
to fresh sheets
a washed head of hair
laundry done
dishes put away
to-do lists finished
honest hearts
your veiny arms
pulling me in
the sweet cavern
my safe place
our legs intertwine
roses bloom on vines
& i put down
my walls & shields—
for i am home

unknown histories

trees planted in lines
creating borders
circular rings
set in time
as family lineages
labeled as leaves while
traditions are forgotten
i wish i could trace all
of your roots
back for you
sadly, history lies
& those in power
will never admit their
wrongdoings
in my lifetime
i hope they do in yours

pillow talk

in the middle of the night
conversations with sleepy sand
locking our eyes are my favorite
private thoughts & dreamt wishes
twirl off our tongues—
sharing secrets only we know
our stolen seconds in time.

sorry is just a word

15

rewiring my brain to stop constantly
saying sorry should not be this
hard—from now on
the only apologizing
i will do is to
myself

moody

hot soggy sidewalks & long drives in
the moody summertime as inside
jokes unravel into whiskey
soaked starry nights &
fingertips trace
bodies
&
goosebumps
multiply & warm
bodies twist together
as diamond droplets of
sweat rain down our spines—
the taste so sweet, you will never forget

have fun

17

it's hard to stomach the reality of time,
please love fiercely, day dream
always & shrug off uncertainty.
i hope you are really
having fun—a life with no regrets
is a life not lived at all.

friendships statistics

i hope you know
when all the hats
you wear weigh
heavy on your head
i will always make sure
your feet are steady
your chin stays high
your belly is full of laughter
your back gets a break—
anything, anywhere, anytime
for a friendship like ours is
what most people long for

heal by the way of the earth

reside in quiet moments
soak your soul in the silence
let rain bathe your toes
dig your feet deep in dirt
remind yourself: everyone
is connected & each one of us
just wants to belong—
for some, it is another person,
others, a place or feeling—
but do not judge anyone's journey
for it could cheapen your own
& what fun would that be?

main character

feelings are heavy
emotions pass
time is permanent
be selfish with whom
you carve out hours for—
people disappoint
avoid those afraid
of accountability
don't settle
when it comes to
backing yourself—
strive to have more fun as a party of one
than with others—
the truest friendship is the one within you
you are the main character,
start acting like it.

sense of myself

21

in loving you, i have learned
to love the dark deep parts
of me—that sounds strange
but it makes sense
to me.